LET'S COOK TOGETHER!

Fun and tasty recipes to make with your KIDS!

Publications International, Ltd.

Pictured on the front cover (*clockwise from top left*): Fruit Kabobs with Raspberry Yogurt Dip (*page 136*), Waffled Burger Sliders (*page 19*), Neon Sponge Cake Tower (*page 170*), Kids' Pizzas (*page 62*), and Chili Cheese Fries (*page 116*).

Pictured on the back cover (*clockwise from top left*): Caramel Apple Nachos (*page 111*), Tic-Tac-Toe Sandwich (*page 26*), Dizzy Dogs (*page 24*), and Guacamole Cones (*page 118*).

Artwork on cover and interior pages © Shutterstock.com.

ISBN: 978-1-64558-608-1

Manufactured in China.

8 7 6 5 4 3 2 1

Microwave Cooking: Microwave ovens vary in wattage. Use the cooking times as guidelines and check for doneness before adding more time.

Let's get social!

 @Publications_International

 @PublicationsInternational

www.pilbooks.com

CONTENTS

INTRODUCTION

There's nothing better than spending quality time with your family. Even getting everyone together for a quick meal can be challenging. But it's so worth it in the long run. Even better is time spent together preparing meals and snacks. Studies have shown that kids who spend time in the kitchen and learn to cook from a young age have improved math and science skills, gain knowledge at problem solving, and tend to become better eaters overall. Learning about ingredient measurements, cooking styles, preparation techniques, and various types of foods are not only fun and exciting but help create lifelong skills that are important in gaining independence in life.

Here, we're offering you the chance to gather up your kids and create meals and snacks that satisfy everyone's palate. Plan what works for you. Pick a weeknight or weekend afternoon to gather, select a theme or allow different individuals to choose the activity, and as a result you'll create great memories in the kitchen. Let us help you get the most out of your time together.

As you navigate through the pages here, keep in mind this book was created for adults and kids to cook together. An adult should always be present when any child is using an appliance or kitchen tool. Supervision is key until skills are fine tuned. Children develop skills at various ages, so make sure your child clearly understands safety rules before attempting tasks on their own.

COOKING SKILLS BY AGE

The chart below is a guide to help you understand ages at which children are capable of accomplishing various tasks.

Ages 3 to 5

wash vegetables, tear lettuce, spoon sauce over casseroles or pizza crusts, stir ingredients, set the table

Ages 6 to 8

weigh and measure ingredients, knead bread, spread icing, beat eggs, mash potatoes, turn oven and appliances on and off

Ages 8 to 12

learn knife skills, roll dough, bread meats and vegetables, follow a recipe, use a can opener

SAFETY TIPS

- Kids should ask for permission before cooking or preparing any foods.
- Everyone should wash hands before touching any food and especially after touching any raw foods.
- Make a habit of tying up hair and long sleeves and wearing an apron to keep clothes clean.
- Clean as you go, place dirty dishes in the sink to keep them away from clean items.
- Keep appliance cords up and away from the sink or any water.
- Use pot holders or oven mitts for when grabbing hot items.
- Practice knife skills. First start with butter knife for young children and slowly graduate as skills are learned and children grow older.
- Store knives and any sharp items properly.
- Keep raw foods away from those foods that have been cooked.
- Wipe up any spills immediately.

> Enjoy your time in the kitchen with your family. As time goes on, you'll find that these times are very precious and create memories you'll share for many years to come.

START OFF YOUR DAY

HARVEST APPLE OATMUG

MAKES
1
SERVING

1 cup water

½ cup old-fashioned oats

½ cup chopped Granny Smith apple

2 tablespoons raisins

1 teaspoon packed brown sugar

¼ teaspoon ground cinnamon

⅛ teaspoon salt

MICROWAVE DIRECTIONS

1. Combine water, oats, apple, raisins, brown sugar, cinnamon and salt in large microwavable mug; mix well.

2. Microwave on HIGH 1½ minutes; stir. Microwave on HIGH 1 minute or until thickened and liquid is absorbed. Let stand 1 to 2 minutes before serving.

STUFFED FRENCH TOAST SANDWICH

MAKES
4
SERVINGS

8 slices whole wheat or white bread

4 thin slices deli ham (about 1 ounce each)

3 eggs

¾ cup milk

1 tablespoon sugar

Butter (optional)

Maple syrup, warmed

1. Place 4 bread slices on baking sheet. Top each with 1 ham slice. Top with remaining bread slices.

2. Whisk eggs, milk and sugar in medium bowl. Pour egg mixture over sandwiches. Let stand 5 minutes, turning once.

3. Spray large skillet with nonstick cooking spray; heat over medium heat. Cook sandwiches in batches, if necessary, 2 minutes on each side or until golden brown. Serve sandwiches with butter, if desired, and syrup.

SERVING SUGGESTION: Cut in half diagonally and serve with fresh fruit on the side.

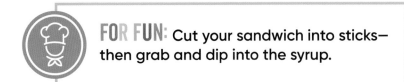

FOR FUN: Cut your sandwich into sticks—then grab and dip into the syrup.

BISCUIT PIZZAS

MAKES
8
SERVINGS

1 package (about 16 ounces) refrigerated flaky biscuits

8 tablespoons tomato sauce

2 slices turkey bacon

¼ cup chopped green bell pepper (optional)

¼ cup chopped onion (optional)

4 eggs, lightly beaten

¼ teaspoon black pepper

½ cup (2 ounces) shredded Cheddar cheese

1. Preheat oven to 375°F. Place biscuits 2 inches apart on large ungreased baking sheet. Make indentation in center of each biscuit. Spoon 1 tablespoon tomato sauce into center.

2. Cook bacon, bell pepper and onion, if desired, in large nonstick skillet over medium-high heat until crisp. Remove bacon to paper towels. Drain drippings from skillet.

3. Spray same skillet with nonstick cooking spray. Add eggs; season with black pepper. Cook, stirring often, about 2 to 3 minutes or until eggs are set.

4. Divide eggs evenly into biscuit centers. Crumble bacon; sprinkle over eggs. Top with cheese. Bake 15 to 17 minutes or until pizza edges are golden brown.

TRY THIS: Substitute other favorite pizza toppings, too. Try mini pepperoni instead of bacon, mozzarella instead of Cheddar cheese.

CHOCOLATE CHERRY PANCAKES

MAKES

20 TO 24

PANCAKES
(6 TO 8 SERVINGS)

- 2 cups all-purpose flour
- 1 cup dried cherries
- ⅔ cup semisweet chocolate chips
- ⅓ cup sugar
- 4½ teaspoons baking powder
- ½ teaspoon baking soda
- ½ teaspoon salt
- 1½ cups milk
- 2 eggs
- ¼ cup (½ stick) butter, melted

1. Combine flour, dried cherries, chocolate chips, sugar, baking powder, baking soda and salt in large bowl; mix well. Beat milk, eggs and butter in medium bowl until well blended.

2. Add milk mixture to flour mixture; stir just until moistened. (Add ¼ to ½ cup additional milk if thinner pancakes are desired.)

3. Heat griddle or large nonstick skillet over medium heat until drop of water sizzles when dropped on surface. Pour batter onto griddle, ¼ cup at a time. Cook 2 to 3 minutes on each side or until golden.

TOP IT OFF: Top your pancakes with whipped cream and additional chocolate chips.

FRUIT AND WAFFLE PARFAIT CUP

MAKES

4

SERVINGS

1 cooked or leftover Belgian waffle, torn into bite-sized pieces

½ cup raspberry jam

½ teaspoon almond extract

1 cup plain or vanilla yogurt

2 cups chopped fresh peaches or thawed frozen peaches

1. Place equal amounts of waffle pieces in each of 4 parfait dishes.

2. Place jam in small microwavable bowl; microwave on HIGH 30 seconds to slightly melt. Stir in almond extract until smooth. Spoon over waffle pieces; top with yogurt and fruit.

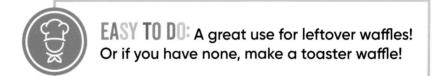

EASY TO DO: A great use for leftover waffles! Or if you have none, make a toaster waffle!

CRUNCHY FRENCH TOAST STICKS

MAKES 6 SERVINGS

6 slices Italian bread (each 1 inch thick, about 3½ to 4 inches in diameter)

4 cups cornflakes, crushed

3 eggs

⅔ cup milk

1 tablespoon sugar

1 teaspoon ground cinnamon

1 teaspoon vanilla

¼ teaspoon ground nutmeg

1 container (6 ounces) vanilla yogurt

¼ cup maple syrup

Ground cinnamon (optional)

1. Preheat oven to 375°F. Lightly spray baking sheet with nonstick cooking spray. Remove crusts from bread, if desired. Cut each bread slice into 3 strips. Place cornflakes on waxed paper.

2. Whisk eggs, milk, sugar, 1 teaspoon cinnamon, vanilla and nutmeg in shallow bowl. Dip bread strips in egg mixture, turning to generously coat all sides. Roll in cornflakes, coating all sides. Place on prepared baking sheet.

3. Bake 25 to 28 minutes or until golden brown, turning sticks after 15 minutes.

4. Meanwhile, combine yogurt and maple syrup in small bowl. Sprinkle with additional cinnamon, if desired. Serve French toast sticks with yogurt mixture.

NO WASTE: Save the crust from the bread in a resealable plastic bag. Feed them outside to birds and ducks—they'll love it!

WRAPS, ROLLS & SANDWICHES

WAFFLED BURGER SLIDERS

MAKES 8 SLIDERS

½ **pound lean ground beef**

½ **teaspoon salt**

Black pepper

8 **slider buns *or* 4 slices bread, cut into quarters and lightly toasted**

1 **tablespoon butter, melted**

Desired toppings: lettuce, tomatoes, cheese, pickles, ketchup

1. Combine beef and salt in large bowl. Season with pepper. Divide into 8 small patties; set aside.

2. Heat waffle maker to medium. Brush buns with melted butter; set aside.

3. Place 4 patties at a time in waffle maker. Cook about 3 minutes or until cooked through. Place 1 patty in each bun, adding desired toppings.

NOTE: If you don't want to use a waffle maker, heat 1 tablespoon oil in large nonstick skillet over medium-high heat. Working in 2 batches, cook patties 2 minutes on each side.

SANDWICH MONSTERS

MAKES
7
SANDWICHES

- 1 package (about 16 ounces) refrigerated jumbo buttermilk biscuits (8 biscuits)
- 1 cup (4 ounces) shredded mozzarella cheese
- ⅓ cup sliced mushrooms
- 2 ounces pepperoni slices (about 35 slices), quartered
- ½ cup pizza sauce, plus additional for dipping
- 1 egg, beaten

1. Preheat oven to 350°F. Line baking sheet with parchment paper or foil.

2. Separate biscuits; set aside 1 biscuit for decorations. Roll out remaining biscuits into 7-inch circles on lightly floured surface.

3. Top half of each circle evenly with cheese, mushrooms, pepperoni and sauce, leaving ½-inch border. Fold dough over filling to form semicircle; seal edges with fork. Brush tops with egg.

4. Split remaining biscuit horizontally and cut each half into 8 (¼-inch) strips. For each sandwich, roll 2 strips of dough into spirals to create eyes. Divide remaining 2 strips of dough into 7 pieces to create noses. Arrange eyes and noses on tops of sandwiches; brush with egg. Place on prepared baking sheet.

5. Bake 20 to 25 minutes or until golden brown. Remove to wire rack to cool 5 minutes. Serve with additional pizza sauce.

GHASTLY: Don't worry about leaking sauce or cheese— it will look like it's coming from the monster's mouth!

VEGGIE PIZZA PITAS

MAKES

4

SERVINGS

2 whole wheat pita bread rounds, cut in half horizontally (to make 4 rounds)

¼ cup pizza sauce

1 teaspoon dried basil

⅛ teaspoon red pepper flakes (optional)

1 cup sliced mushrooms

½ cup thinly sliced green bell pepper

½ cup thinly sliced red onion

1 cup (4 ounces) shredded part-skim mozzarella cheese

2 teaspoons grated Parmesan cheese

1. Preheat oven to 475°F.

2. Arrange pita rounds, rough sides up, in single layer on large nonstick baking sheet. Spread 1 tablespoon pizza sauce evenly over each pita round to within ¼ inch of edge. Sprinkle with basil and red pepper flakes, if desired. Top with mushrooms, bell pepper and onion. Sprinkle with mozzarella cheese.

3. Bake 5 minutes or until mozzarella cheese is melted. Sprinkle ½ teaspoon Parmesan cheese over each pita round.

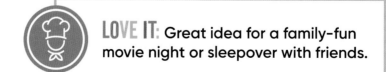

LOVE IT: Great idea for a family-fun movie night or sleepover with friends.

DIZZY DOGS

MAKES
12
SERVINGS

12 hot dogs

1 package (about 11 ounces) refrigerated breadstick dough (12 breadsticks)

1 egg white

Sesame seeds and poppy seeds

Mustard, ketchup and barbecue sauce (optional)

1. Preheat oven to 375°F.

2. Wrap each hot dog with 1 piece dough in spiral pattern. Brush with egg white and sprinkle with sesame seeds and poppy seeds. Place on ungreased baking sheet.

3. Bake 12 to 15 minutes or until light golden brown. Serve with condiments for dipping, if desired.

PEANUT BUTTER-APPLE WRAPS

MAKES

4

SERVINGS

¾ cup creamy peanut butter

4 (7-inch) whole wheat or spinach tortillas

¾ cup finely chopped apple

⅓ cup shredded carrot

⅓ cup low-fat granola without raisins

1 tablespoon toasted wheat germ

Spread peanut butter on one side of each tortilla. Sprinkle apple, carrot, granola and wheat germ evenly over each tortilla. Roll up tightly; cut in half. Serve immediately or wrap in plastic wrap and refrigerate until ready to serve.

TIC-TAC-TOE SANDWICH

MAKES

1

SANDWICH

- 2 teaspoons mayonnaise
- 1 slice whole wheat sandwich bread
- 1 slice white sandwich bread
- 1 slice (1 ounce) cheese
- 1 slice deli ham
- 3 green or black olives

1. Spread 1 teaspoon mayonnaise on each bread slice. Layer cheese and ham on 1 bread slice. Top with remaining bread slice.

2. Trim crust from sandwich. Cut sandwich into 9 squares by cutting into thirds in each direction. Turn alternating pieces over to form checkerboard pattern.

3. Thinly slice 1 olive to form 'O's. Cut remaining 2 olives into strips. Place olive pieces on sandwich squares to form 'X's and 'O's.

TRY THIS: Such a fun way to eat lunch. You can also make your 'X's and 'O's using thin cucumber slices and baby carrot sticks.

BBQ TURKEY MINIS

MAKES
12
MINI
BURGERS

- ½ cup panko bread crumbs
- ½ cup barbecue sauce, divided
- 1 egg, beaten
- 1 pound 93% lean ground turkey
- 1 package (12 ounces) Hawaiian bread rolls, split horizontally
- Lettuce
- Tomato slices
- 3 slices American cheese, quartered

1. Generously grease grid. Prepare grill for direct cooking over high heat.

2. Combine panko, ¼ cup barbecue sauce and egg in medium bowl; mix well. Add turkey; mix just until combined. Shape into 12 small ½-inch-thick patties (¼ cup per patty).

3. Grill* patties, covered, 8 to 10 minutes, turning once. Brush with remaining ¼ cup barbecue sauce during last minute of cooking.

4. Serve patties on rolls with lettuce, tomato and cheese.

*Centers of burgers should reach 160°F before being removed from grill; internal temperature will continue to rise to 165°F upon standing.

KIDS LOVE IT: This makes a fun recipe for your next backyard BBQ.

MR. FROGGY

MAKES

4

SERVINGS

1 avocado

Salt and black pepper

Juice of 1 lime

4 ounces deli ham or turkey

4 corn tortillas

Grape tomatoes, sliced

1. Mash avocado in small bowl; season with salt and pepper. Stir in lime juice. Keep covered. Cut out 4 tongue shapes from 1 slice of ham. Shred remaining ham.

2. Working with 1 tortilla at a time, microwave tortillas on HIGH 20 to 30 seconds to soften. Fold tortilla in half; cut long ovals for eyes being careful to leave bottom edge of eye intact. Spread avocado mixture over one half of tortilla; top with shredded ham. Fold over, leaving eyes sticking up.

3. Heat large nonstick skillet over medium-high heat. Cook tortillas 1 to 2 minutes per side until heated through and lightly browned. Place on serving plate and add ham tongues and tomato slices for eyes.

FUN FOR ALL: Grab a potato masher and have your little one mash the avocado. Even the smallest of kids can help.

HAM, APPLE AND CHEESE TURNOVERS

MAKES

6

SERVINGS

1¼ cups chopped cooked ham

¾ cup finely chopped peeled apple

¾ cup (3 ounces) shredded Cheddar cheese

1 tablespoon brown mustard

1 package (about 14 ounces) refrigerated pizza dough

1. Preheat oven to 400°F. Line baking sheet with parchment paper or spray with nonstick cooking spray.

2. Combine ham, apple, cheese and mustard in medium bowl; mix well.

3. Roll out dough into 15×10-inch rectangle on lightly floured surface. Cut into 6 (5-inch) squares. Divide ham mixture evenly among squares. Moisten edges with water; fold dough over filling to form triangles. Press edges with fork to seal. Place on prepared baking sheet; prick tops of each turnover with fork.

4. Bake about 15 minutes or until golden brown. Serve warm or cool on wire rack 1 hour.

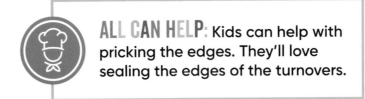

ALL CAN HELP: Kids can help with pricking the edges. They'll love sealing the edges of the turnovers.

BAVARIAN PRETZEL SANDWICHES

MAKES
4
SANDWICHES

4 frozen soft pretzels, thawed

1 tablespoon German mustard

2 teaspoons mayonnaise

8 slices Black Forest ham

4 slices (1 ounce each) Gouda cheese

1 tablespoon water

Coarse pretzel salt

1. Preheat oven to 350°F. Line baking sheet with parchment paper.

2. Carefully slice each pretzel in half crosswise using serrated knife. Combine mustard and mayonnaise in small bowl. Spread mustard mixture onto bottom halves of pretzels. Top with 2 slices ham, 1 slice cheese and top halves of pretzels.

3. Place sandwiches on prepared baking sheet. Brush tops of sandwiches with water; sprinkle with salt. Bake 8 minutes or until cheese is melted.

GREAT IDEA: Also make cold pretzel sandwiches. Bake pretzels according to package directions. When they are cool enough to handle, slice them and top with sandwich fillings.

QUICK WAFFLED QUESADILLAS

MAKES
1
SERVING

2 (6-inch) flour tortillas

⅓ cup (1½ ounces) shredded Cheddar cheese or Monterey Jack cheese

1 small plum tomato, chopped

Salt and black pepper

½ ripe medium avocado, chopped

1 to 2 tablespoons chopped fresh cilantro

Juice of ½ lime

1. Preheat waffle maker to medium; coat both sides of each tortilla with nonstick cooking spray.

2. Top tortilla with cheese, tomato, salt, pepper and other tortilla. Place on waffle maker; close, pressing down slightly. Cook 2 to 3 minutes or until golden brown and cheese has melted.

3. Carefully remove tortilla. Cut into 4 sections, using a serrated knife. Top with avocado, cilantro and lime juice.

BRING IT ON: Waffling makes this fun, but you can make this without a waffle maker, too! Just heat for 1 minute in the microwave.

TRY THIS: Let your little ones stir in some sliced hot dogs or vegetables near the end of cooking. Cover; cook until heated through.

TUNA PIES

MAKES

4

SERVINGS

1 can (8 ounces) refrigerated crescent roll dough

1 can (about 5 ounces) water-packed tuna, drained

1 tablespoon mayonnaise

1 cup (4 ounces) shredded Cheddar cheese

1. Preheat oven to 400°F. Separate crescent dough into triangles; press 2 perforated triangles together to form 4 rectangles. Press rectangles into bottoms and up sides of 4 ovenproof mugs or ramekins.

2. Combine tuna and mayonnaise in small bowl; mix gently. Spoon tuna mixture evenly over dough; sprinkle with cheese.

3. Bake 10 minutes or until dough is golden brown. Let cool slightly before serving.

TRY THIS: Add your favorite vegetables, like broccoli or peas, to this recipe. Or try other types of cheese, like mozzarella or Swiss.

CHILI CON CORNY

MAKES
4
SERVINGS

- 1 tablespoon vegetable oil
- ½ cup finely chopped onion
- 1 pound ground turkey
- 1 can (about 15 ounces) kidney beans, rinsed and drained
- 1 can (about 14 ounces) diced tomatoes
- 1 can (11 ounces) corn, drained
- 1 can (8 ounces) tomato sauce
- 2 teaspoons chili seasoning mix or taco seasoning mix
- 1 teaspoon salt
- 1 teaspoon ground cumin
- ¾ cup (3 ounces) shredded Cheddar cheese
- 2 cups corn chips

1. Heat oil in large skillet over medium heat. Add onion; cook and stir 2 minutes. Add turkey; cook until no longer pink, stirring to break up meat.

2. Stir in beans, tomatoes, corn, tomato sauce, chili seasoning mix, salt and cumin. Bring mixture to a simmer; cook 10 minutes, stirring frequently.

3. Serve chili with cheese and corn chips.

FAVORITE MEAL: Let kids add their own cheese and corn chips. The more they get involved, the more likely they'll be to eat their creation.

MAC & CHEESE BITES

MAKES ABOUT **2** DOZEN

3 packages (3 ounces each) ramen noodles, any flavor, divided*

8 ounces pasteurized process cheese product

1 cup (4 ounces) shredded Cheddar cheese

1 teaspoon salt

½ teaspoon ground red pepper

Vegetable oil

*Discard seasoning packets.

1. Prepare 2 packages ramen according to package directions; drain and return to saucepan.

2. Stir in cheese product, Cheddar cheese, salt and ground red pepper. Let stand 10 to 15 minutes.

3. Finely crush remaining packet of ramen noodles in food processor or blender. Put crumbs in pie pan. Using hands, shape cheese mixture into 1-inch balls; roll in ramen crumbs. Flatten slightly.

4. Heat about ½ to 1 inch oil in large skillet. Add bites, a few at a time; cook 1½ minutes per side or until golden brown. Remove from skillet; drain on paper towels.

FUN TO DO: You can also crush the noodles by putting them in a large resealable storage bag and crushing them with a rolling pin.

PIZZA MEATBALL AND NOODLE SOUP

MAKES
4
SERVINGS

- 1 can (about 14 ounces) beef broth
- ½ cup chopped onion
- ½ cup chopped carrot
- 2 ounces uncooked whole wheat spaghetti, broken into 2- to 3-inch pieces
- 1 cup zucchini slices, cut in half
- 8 ounces frozen fully cooked Italian-style meatballs, thawed
- 1 can (8 ounces) tomato sauce
- ½ cup (2 ounces) shredded mozzarella cheese

1. Combine broth, onion, carrot and pasta in large saucepan. Bring to a boil over medium-high heat. Reduce heat to low. Simmer, covered, 3 minutes.

2. Add zucchini, meatballs and tomato sauce to broth mixture; return to a boil. Reduce heat to low. Simmer, covered, 8 to 9 minutes or until meatballs are heated through and spaghetti is tender, stirring occasionally. Ladle into serving bowls; sprinkle with cheese.

ON THE SIDE: Serve with garlic or cheesy bread for dipping.

BIG KID SHRIMP

MAKES

4

SERVINGS

- ½ **cup plain dry bread crumbs**
- ¼ **cup grated Parmesan cheese**
- ½ **teaspoon paprika**
- ½ **teaspoon salt**
- ⅛ **teaspoon black pepper**
- 2 **tablespoons butter, melted**
- 1 **pound large raw shrimp, peeled and deveined**
- ½ **cup mayonnaise**
- ½ **cup ketchup**
- 1 **tablespoon sweet pickle relish**

1. Preheat oven to 400°F. Line a jelly-roll pan with foil; spray with nonstick cooking spray.

2. Combine bread crumbs, Parmesan cheese, paprika, salt and pepper in large bowl. Add melted butter; mix well. Rinse shrimp under cold water, drain, and toss with bread crumb mixture. Place shrimp on prepared jelly-roll pan in single layer. Bake 15 minutes or until lightly browned and cooked through.

3. Combine mayonnaise, ketchup and relish in small bowl. Serve with shrimp.

FINGER FOOD: Keeping the tails on make them easier for kids to dip and eat.

KIDS' PIZZAS

MAKES
2
PIZZAS

1 package (10 ounces)
    8-inch mini pizza crusts

1 can (about 14 ounces)
    pizza sauce

½ teaspoon Italian
    seasoning

½ cup (2 ounces) shredded
    mozzarella cheese

1 package (about 3 ounces)
    sliced pepperoni

1. Preheat oven to 450°F. Line baking sheet or pizza pans with parchment paper.

2. Place pizza crusts on prepared pan. Spread sauce evenly over crusts. Sprinkle with Italian seasoning and cheese. Create a face or other design with pepperoni slices.

3. Bake 8 to 12 minutes or until cheese is melted and crusts are lightly browned.

TRY THIS: Add sliced olives, bell pepper pieces and even pineapple tidbits to your pizza, too!

FALAFEL NUGGETS

MAKES
12
SERVINGS

FALAFEL

- 2 cans (about 15 ounces each) chickpeas
- ½ cup whole wheat flour
- ½ cup chopped fresh parsley
- 1 egg, beaten
- ⅓ cup lemon juice
- ¼ cup minced onion
- 2 tablespoons minced garlic
- 2 teaspoons ground cumin
- ½ teaspoon salt
- ½ teaspoon ground red pepper or red pepper flakes

SAUCE

- 2½ cups tomato sauce
- ⅓ cup tomato paste
- 2 tablespoons lemon juice
- 2 teaspoons sugar
- 1 teaspoon onion powder
- ½ teaspoon salt
- ½ cup canola oil

1. Preheat oven to 400°F. Spray baking sheet with nonstick cooking spray.

2. Drain chickpeas, reserving ¼ cup liquid. Combine chickpeas, reserved ¼ cup liquid, flour, parsley, egg, lemon juice, onion, garlic, cumin, ½ teaspoon salt and ground red pepper in food processor or blender; process until well blended. Shape into 36 (1-inch) balls; place 1 to 2 inches apart on prepared baking sheet. Refrigerate 15 minutes.

3. Meanwhile, combine tomato sauce, tomato paste, 2 tablespoons lemon juice, sugar, onion powder and ½ teaspoon salt in medium saucepan. Simmer over medium-low heat 20 minutes; keep warm.

4. Heat oil in large nonstick skillet over medium-high heat to 350°F. Fry* falafel in batches until browned. Place on baking sheet; bake 8 to 10 minutes. Serve with warm sauce.

*Falafel can also be baked. Spray balls lightly with nonstick cooking spray. Bake on baking sheet 15 to 20 minutes, turning once.

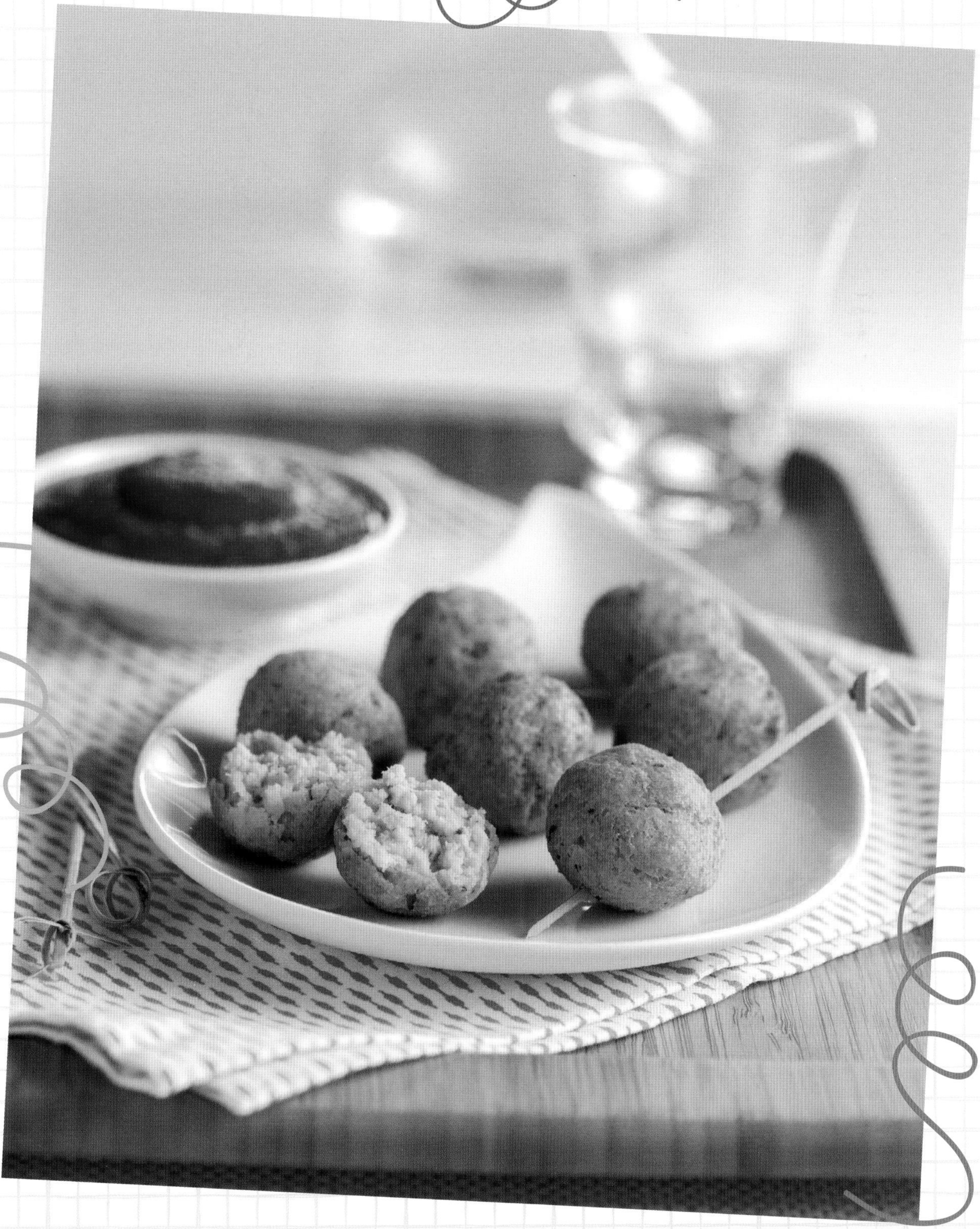

TASTY TORTELLINI SALAD

MAKES

3

SERVINGS

8 ounces refrigerated cheese-filled tortellini or cheese-filled cappelletti

1½ cups broccoli florets

1 cup sliced carrots

⅔ cup Caesar salad dressing

½ cup grape tomatoes, halved

2 tablespoons sliced green onion

3 tablespoons toasted soy nuts or sunflower seeds

1. Cook pasta according to package directions; drain. Rinse with cold water; drain well.

2. Combine pasta, broccoli, carrots, salad dressing, tomatoes and green onion in large bowl. Gently toss. Cover and refrigerate 2 hours or until well chilled. Sprinkle with soy nuts; serve immediately.

TO GO: Pack this salad up in a small thermos. What a great school lunch!

SALMON IN THE WILD

MAKES

4

SERVINGS

1 package (6 ounces) long grain and wild rice mix

1 tablespoon butter or margarine, cut into small pieces

½ cup shredded carrot

2 cups boiling water

1 pound salmon fillets, skin removed

⅓ cup teriyaki sauce

1 sliced orange (optional)

1. Preheat oven to 350°F. Pour rice and contents of seasoning packet into 8-inch square baking dish. Dot rice with butter and top with carrot. Pour boiling water into baking dish.

2. Cut salmon into 8 pieces and evenly space on top of rice mixture. Cover dish with foil and bake 20 minutes. Remove foil; bake 5 minutes longer.

3. Spoon rice and salmon onto serving plates; drizzle salmon with teriyaki sauce. Garnish with orange slices.

LOVE IT: Salmon has a mild flavor which many kids prefer over other types of fish. Plus, the teriyaki sauce adds a sweet touch that entices them even more.

NUTTY CHICKEN AND MANDARIN ORANGE SLAW

MAKES

4

SERVINGS

2 cups chopped cooked chicken (about 4 ounces)

1 cup broccoli slaw mix or coleslaw mix

1 can (11 ounces) mandarin oranges in light syrup, drained

¼ cup coleslaw dressing

¼ cup toasted wheat germ (optional)

¼ cup chopped peanuts

1. Combine chicken, coleslaw mix, oranges and dressing in medium bowl.

2. Cover and refrigerate until ready to serve. Stir in wheat germ, if desired, and peanuts; serve immediately.

 **GREAT IDEA:** Serve in mini pita pockets. Delicious!

SLOPPY JOE'S BUN BUGGY

MAKES

4

SERVINGS

- 4 hot dog buns (not split)
- 16 thin slices cucumber or zucchini
- 24 matchstick-size carrot strips, 1 inch long
- 4 black olives or pimiento-stuffed olives
- 1 package (10 ounces) ground turkey
- 1¼ cups pasta sauce
- ½ cup chopped broccoli stems
- 2 teaspoons prepared mustard
- ½ teaspoon Worcestershire sauce
- Dash salt
- Dash black pepper
- 4 small pretzel twists

1. Hollow out hot dog buns. Use toothpick to make 4 holes in sides of each bun to attach "wheels." Use toothpick to make 1 hole in center of each cucumber slice; push carrot strip through hole. Press into holes in buns, making "wheels" on buns.

2. Cut each olive in half horizontally. Use toothpick to make 2 holes in one end of each bun to attach "headlights." Use carrot strips to attach olives to buns, making "headlights."

3. Spray large nonstick skillet with nonstick cooking spray. Cook and stir turkey in skillet over medium heat until no longer pink. Stir in pasta sauce, broccoli stems, mustard, Worcestershire sauce, salt and pepper; heat through.

4. Spoon turkey mixture into hollowed-out buns. Press pretzel twist into ground turkey mixture, making "windshield" on each buggy.

PICK A SIDE

WHAT A GRAPE SALAD

MAKES

4

SERVINGS

1½ cups green and/or red seedless grapes, halved

1 red apple (such as Gala, Jonathon or Braeburn), cored and diced

½ cup finely diced celery

1 tablespoon golden raisins

½ cup mayonnaise

2 tablespoons plain low-fat yogurt

2 tablespoons crushed cereal

1. Combine grapes, apple, celery and raisins in medium bowl.

2. Whisk mayonnaise and yogurt in small bowl. Gently stir into grape mixture. (Salad may be made up to 1 day ahead. Seal in airtight container and refrigerate until serving time.) Sprinkle each serving with cereal.

FRUIT & NUT QUINOA

MAKES
6
SERVINGS

- 1 cup uncooked quinoa
- 2 cups water
- 2 tablespoons finely grated orange peel, plus additional for garnish
- ¼ cup fresh orange juice
- 2 teaspoons olive oil
- ½ teaspoon salt
- ¼ teaspoon ground cinnamon
- ⅓ cup dried cranberries
- ⅓ cup toasted pistachio nuts*

*To toast pistachios, spread in single layer in heavy skillet. Cook and stir over medium heat 1 to 2 minutes or until nuts are lightly browned.

1. Place quinoa in fine-mesh strainer; rinse well under cold running water.

2. Bring 2 cups water to a boil in medium saucepan over high heat; stir in quinoa. Reduce heat to low; cover and simmer 10 to 15 minutes or until quinoa is tender and water is absorbed. Stir in 2 tablespoons orange peel.

3. Whisk orange juice, oil, salt and cinnamon in small bowl. Pour over quinoa; gently toss to coat. Fold in cranberries and pistachios. Serve warm or at room temperature. Garnish with additional orange peel.

KID APPROVED: Quinoa is a small but mighty food packed with nutrients. It soaks up other flavors—so versatile. Kids love it!

CRUNCH A BUNCH SALAD

MAKES

4

SERVINGS

- 2 tablespoons honey or sugar
- 1 tablespoon vegetable oil
- 1 tablespoon apple cider vinegar
- ½ teaspoon soy sauce or lemon juice
- 1 cup sugar snap peas, trimmed
- 1 carrot, peeled and thinly sliced
- 1 stalk celery, sliced
- 3 radishes, thinly sliced
- 4 cherry tomatoes, cut into quarters
- 4 teaspoons sliced almonds

1. Whisk honey, oil, vinegar and soy sauce in small bowl until well blended.

2. Arrange vegetables, except tomatoes, in 4 bowls. Top with tomatoes and almonds. Drizzle with dressing or serve on the side for dipping.

GO FOR VARIETY: Try other veggies in this salad. In fact, try to create a rainbow of colors.

SMASHED POTATOES

MAKES
4
SERVINGS

4 medium russet potatoes (about 1½ pounds), peeled and cut into ¼-inch cubes

⅓ cup milk

2 tablespoons sour cream

1 tablespoon minced onion

½ teaspoon salt

¼ teaspoon black pepper

⅛ teaspoon garlic powder (optional)

Chopped fresh chives or French fried onions (optional)

1. Bring large saucepan of lightly salted water to a boil. Add potatoes; cook 15 to 20 minutes or until fork-tender. Drain and return to saucepan.

2. Slightly mash potatoes. Stir in milk, sour cream, minced onion, salt, pepper and garlic powder, if desired. Mash until desired texture is reached, leaving potatoes chunky. Cook 5 minutes over low heat or until heated through, stirring occasionally. Top with chives, if desired.

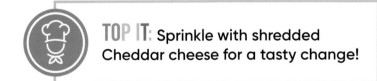 **TOP IT:** Sprinkle with shredded Cheddar cheese for a tasty change!

LAYERED TACO SALAD

MAKES
4
SERVINGS

- ½ pound ground beef
- 1½ teaspoons chili powder
- 1½ teaspoons ground cumin, divided
- ½ cup picante sauce
- 1 teaspoon sugar
- 6 cups shredded romaine lettuce
- 2 plum tomatoes, seeded and diced
- ½ cup chopped green onions
- ¼ cup chopped fresh cilantro
- 28 nacho-flavored baked tortilla chips, crumbled (2 ounces)
- ½ cup sour cream
- ½ cup (2 ounces) shredded sharp Cheddar cheese or Mexican cheese blend

1. Spray medium nonstick skillet with nonstick cooking spray; heat over medium-high heat. Brown beef 3 to 5 minutes, stirring to break up meat. Drain fat. Stir in chili powder and 1 teaspoon cumin. Let cool.

2. Combine picante sauce, sugar and remaining ½ teaspoon cumin in small bowl.

3. Place lettuce in 11×7-inch casserole. Layer with beef, tomatoes, green onions, cilantro and chips. Top with sour cream; sprinkle with cheese. Spoon picante sauce mixture on top.

MUD PUDDLE PIE

MAKES
12
SERVINGS

1 package (about 16 ounces) refrigerated chocolate chip cookie dough

Red, orange and yellow decorating icings

¼ cup chocolate chips, melted

2 tablespoons unsweetened cocoa powder

1 can (15¾ ounces) chocolate pudding

Gummy worms or gummy insects

1. Preheat oven to 350°F. Remove dough from wrapper, keeping log shape. Cut off 1½-inch portion of dough. Place remaining dough in large bowl; set aside.

2. Shape small dough portion into 3 to 4 leaves. Place 2 inches apart on ungreased cookie sheet. Bake 4 to 6 minutes or until edges are lightly browned. Remove to wire rack; cool completely. Decorate with icings as shown. Place chocolate in small resealable food storage bag; seal. Cut off small corner of bag; pipe melted chocolate onto leaves for veins. Let stand until set.

3. Generously grease 12-inch pizza pan. Add cocoa to remaining dough in bowl; beat at medium speed of electric mixer until well blended. Press dough into prepared pan, leaving about ¾-inch space between dough and edge of pan. Bake 9 to 11 minutes or until center is set. Cool completely in pan on wire rack. Run spatula between cookie crust and pan after 10 to 15 minutes to loosen.

4. Spread pudding over crust to within 1 inch of edge. Top with gummy worms and leaf cookies. Cut into wedges to serve.

GIVE THANKS CORNUCOPIAS

MAKES

8

FAVORS OR PLACE CARDS

8 ice cream waffle or sugar cones

3 ounces semisweet chocolate, melted

Assorted fall candies

SUPPLIES

8 (2×¾-inch) pieces lightweight cardboard (optional)

1. Dip edges of cones into melted chocolate; let stand on wire racks or waxed paper until chocolate is firm. Place each cone on its side; fill with candy.

2. To make place cards, write names on pieces of cardboard. Attach to cones with melted chocolate.

COOKIE GOBBLERS

MAKES

4

SERVINGS

- 4 **marshmallow puff cookies**
- 2 **striped shortbread ring cookies**
  Melted semisweet chocolate
- 4 **candy corn**

1. Cut down into each marshmallow cookie halfway between center and edge. Starting in back, cut horizontally toward the first cut. Dip the knife in hot water and dry it before each cut. Discard the pieces.

2. Cut the striped cookies in half. Attach 1 striped cookie half to the cut edge of each marshmallow cookie with melted chocolate for the tail.

3. Attach 1 candy corn to the front of each turkey with melted chocolate for the head. Create eyes with dots of melted chocolate.

AMERICAN FLAG PIZZAS

MAKES
24
SERVINGS

2 packages (about 14 ounces each) refrigerated pizza crust

2 cups prepared pizza sauce

1⅓ cups shredded sharp Cheddar cheese

12 cheese sticks or string cheese (about 1 ounce each), quartered lengthwise (48 pieces total)

25 slices pepperoni, quartered

1. Preheat oven to 400°F. Lightly coat 2 (17×11-inch) nonstick baking sheets with nonstick cooking spray.

2. Unroll pizza crusts on prepared baking sheets. Starting at center, press dough with hands to edges of baking sheets. Bake on center oven rack 8 minutes.

3. Spread 1 cup pizza sauce over each crust. Sprinkle ⅔ cup Cheddar cheese on upper left quarter of each pizza. Arrange 24 cheese strips, end to end, on each pizza to resemble stripes of American flag. Place 50 pepperoni quarters on top of Cheddar cheese to resemble stars.

4. Bake pizzas on center oven rack, one at a time, 8 minutes or until cheese is melted and edges are golden brown. (Do not overbake.)

SPAGHETTI AND EYEBALLS

MAKES

6 TO 8

SERVINGS

- 1 pound ground beef
- ½ cup bread crumbs (plain or seasoned)
- ⅓ cup milk
- 1 egg
- 2 tablespoons finely chopped onion
- ½ teaspoon garlic salt
- 1 jar (16 ounces) large, pimiento-stuffed olives
- 8 ounces spaghetti, uncooked
- 1 jar (16 ounces) pasta sauce, heated (2 cups)
- Roasted red pepper slices (optional)

1. Preheat oven to 400°F. Spray baking sheet with nonstick cooking spray.

2. Combine ground beef, bread crumbs, milk, egg, onion and garlic salt in medium bowl; mix until blended. Shape mixture into 12 (2-inch) balls and place on prepared baking sheet. Press olive, pimiento end up, into each meatball to form eyeballs. Bake 15 minutes or until meatballs are browned and cooked through.

3. Meanwhile, prepare spaghetti according to package directions. Drain.

4. Toss hot spaghetti with pasta sauce in large bowl. Top each pasta serving with eyeballs and red pepper slice for tongue, if desired. Serve hot.

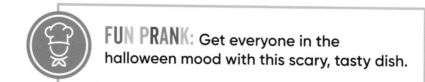

FUN PRANK: Get everyone in the halloween mood with this scary, tasty dish.

SANTA'S COOKIE PIZZA

MAKES
16
WEDGES

- ¾ cup (1½ sticks) butter, softened
- ¾ cup sugar
- 3 egg yolks
- 1 teaspoon vanilla
- 1½ cups all-purpose flour
- ¼ cup unsweetened cocoa powder
- ¼ teaspoon salt
- 1 package (12 ounces) white chocolate chips
- ½ cup plus 1 tablespoon sweetened condensed milk, divided
- 1 cup mini pretzel twists
- 1 cup red and green gumdrops
- ½ cup chopped peanuts
- ½ cup red and green candy-coated chocolate pieces

1. Preheat oven to 350°F. Lightly spray 12-inch round pizza pan with nonstick cooking spray.

2. Beat butter and sugar in large bowl with electric mixer at medium speed 1 minute. Beat in egg yolks and vanilla until well blended. Sift flour, cocoa and salt into small bowl. Add to butter mixture; beat just until combined.

3. Press dough into prepared pan, building up edge slightly. Refrigerate at least 15 minutes. Prick holes all over dough with fork. Bake 18 to 20 minutes or until firm. Remove to wire rack to cool slightly.

4. Heat white chocolate chips and ½ cup sweetened condensed milk in medium saucepan over low heat until chocolate is melted, stirring constantly. Reserve one fourth of chocolate mixture; spread remaining mixture evenly over crust. Immediately sprinkle with pretzels, gumdrops, peanuts and chocolate pieces, pressing down gently to adhere.

5. Combine remaining 1 tablespoon condensed milk and reserved chocolate mixture; stir over low heat until blended. Drizzle over pizza. Cool completely on wire rack before cutting into wedges. Store in airtight container.

ROARING CAMPFIRES

MAKES
ABOUT

3

DOZEN
COOKIES

1 package (about 16 ounces) refrigerated peanut butter cookie dough

¾ cup all-purpose flour

2 tablespoons unsweetened cocoa powder

2 cups broken thin pretzel sticks

1 tube (4¼ ounces) yellow star icing with decorating tip

1 tube (4¼ ounces) orange star icing with decorating tip

1. Let dough stand at room temperature about 15 minutes. Preheat oven to 350°F. Lightly grease cookie sheets.

2. Beat dough, flour and cocoa in large bowl until well blended. Shape dough into 1-inch balls; place 2 inches apart on prepared cookie sheets.

3. Bake about 7 minutes or until set. Immediately press pretzel pieces into sides of cookies to resemble campfire logs. Remove to wire racks; cool completely.

4. Using decorating tips, pipe yellow and orange icing onto cooled cookies to resemble flames.

CAMPING FUN: A perfect treat for scouting events.

HALLOWEEN HEDGEHOGS

MAKES
22
CUPCAKES

1 package (about 18 ounces) chocolate cake mix, plus ingredients to prepare mix

1 container (16 ounces) chocolate frosting

White chocolate chips

Black jelly beans, cut into halves

Black decorating gel (optional)

3 cups candy corn

1. Preheat oven to 350°F. Line 22 standard (2½-inch) muffin cups with paper baking cups. Prepare cake mix according to package directions. Spoon batter into prepared muffin cups, filling two-thirds full.

2. Bake 20 minutes or until toothpick inserted into centers comes out clean. Cool in pans 10 minutes. Remove to wire racks; cool completely.

3. Frost cupcakes. Arrange white chips and jelly bean half on one side of each cupcake to create face; pipe dot of frosting or decorating gel onto each eye. Arrange candy corn around face and all over each cupcake.

PRICK IT: Kids love poking their hedgehogs with the candy corn.

PARTY POPCORN

MAKES

6

QUARTS

¼ **cup vegetable oil**

½ **cup unpopped popcorn kernels**

1 **teaspoon fine sea salt or popcorn salt**

4 **ounces almond bark,* chopped**

Rainbow nonpareils

*Look for almond bark by the chocolate chips in the baking aisle of the grocery store.

1. Line 2 sheet pans with parchment paper.

2. Heat oil in large 6-quart saucepan over medium-high heat 1 minute. Add popcorn. Cover tightly with lid and cook 2 to 3 minutes or until popcorn slows to about 1 second between pops, carefully shaking pan occasionally.

3. Spread popcorn on prepared sheet pans; immediately sprinkle with salt and toss gently to blend.

4. Melt almond bark according to package directions. Drizzle over popcorn; sprinkle with nonpareils. Let stand until set.

GREAT IDEA: Pack this popcorn up in a small resealable bag tied with a ribbon—great for teacher gifts, bake sales or other special events.

CHILI CHEESE FRIES

MAKES

4

SERVINGS

1½ pounds ground beef

1 medium onion, chopped

2 cloves garlic, minced

½ cup water

2 tablespoons chili powder

2 tablespoons tomato paste

Salt and black pepper

1 package (32 ounces) frozen French fries

1 jar (15 ounces) cheese sauce, heated

Sour cream and chopped green onions (optional)

1. Brown beef, onion and garlic in large skillet over medium-high heat 6 to 8 minutes, stirring to break up meat. Drain fat.

2. Stir water, chili powder and tomato paste into beef mixture. Simmer, stirring occasionally, 20 minutes or until most liquid has evaporated. Season with salt and pepper.

3. Meanwhile, bake French fries according to package directions.

4. Divide French fries evenly among bowls. Top evenly with chili and cheese sauce. Garnish with sour cream and green onions.

CRUNCHY RAMEN CHOW

MAKES ABOUT **8** CUPS

4 packages (3 ounces each) ramen noodles, any flavor*

1 cup semisweet chocolate chips

1 cup butterscotch chips

¾ cup creamy peanut butter

¼ cup (½ stick) butter

1½ cups powdered sugar

*Discard seasoning packets.

1. Break noodles into bite-size pieces; place in large bowl.

2. Combine chocolate chips, butterscotch chips, peanut butter and butter in medium microwavable bowl. Microwave on HIGH 1 minute; stir. Continue to microwave at 30-second intervals, stirring until smooth.

3. Pour chocolate mixture over noodles; toss to coat evenly.

4. Place powdered sugar in 1-gallon resealable food storage bag. Add noodle mixture; shake until well coated. Spread in single layer on waxed or parchment paper to cool. Store in airtight container.

YUMMY: **Whip up a batch in no time—great for parties and everyday snacking!**

SNAKE SNACKS

MAKES

2

SERVINGS

2 **small ripe bananas**

1 **tablespoon fresh lemon juice**

10 **to 12 medium strawberries, hulled**

2 **small strawberries, hulled**

1 **slice kiwi (optional)**

1. Peel and cut bananas crosswise into ¼-inch slices. Place in medium bowl; toss gently with lemon juice to prevent bananas from turning brown.

2. Leave 2 medium strawberries whole; cut remaining medium strawberries crosswise into ¼-inch slices.

3. Place whole strawberries on serving plates for heads; alternate banana and strawberry slices behind heads to form snakes. Arrange small strawberries at ends of snakes.

4. Cut 4 small pieces of banana for eyes and pieces of strawberries for tongue; arrange on snake heads. Use toothpick to place kiwi seed in center of each eye, if desired.

NOTE: Try to choose strawberries that are about the same diameter as the banana so all the fruit slices that make up the snake will be close to the same width.

MOZZARELLA STICKS

MAKES
4 TO **6**
SERVINGS

- ¼ cup all-purpose flour
- 2 eggs
- 1 tablespoon water
- 1 cup plain dry bread crumbs
- 2 teaspoons Italian seasoning
- ½ teaspoon salt
- ½ teaspoon garlic powder
- 1 package (12 ounces) string cheese (12 sticks)
- Vegetable oil for frying
- 1 cup marinara or pizza sauce, heated

1. Place flour in shallow bowl. Whisk eggs and water in another shallow bowl. Combine bread crumbs, Italian seasoning, salt and garlic powder in third shallow bowl.

2. Coat each piece of cheese with flour. Dip in egg mixture, letting excess drip back into bowl. Roll in bread crumb mixture to coat. Dip again in egg mixture and roll again in bread crumb mixture. Place on plate; refrigerate until ready to cook.

3. Heat 2 inches of oil in large saucepan over medium-high heat to 350°F; adjust heat to maintain temperature during frying. Add cheese sticks; cook about 1 minute or until golden brown. Drain on wire rack. Serve with warm marinara sauce for dipping.

FAN FAVORITE: These ooey-gooey treats taste even better when homemade from scratch.

LOADED BANANA BREAD

MAKES 1 LOAF

6 tablespoons (¾ stick) butter, softened

⅓ cup granulated sugar

⅓ cup packed brown sugar

2 eggs

3 ripe bananas, mashed

½ teaspoon vanilla

1½ cups all-purpose flour

2½ teaspoons baking powder

¼ teaspoon salt

1 can (8 ounces) crushed pineapple, drained

⅓ cup flaked coconut

¼ cup mini chocolate chips

⅓ cup chopped walnuts (optional)

1. Preheat oven to 350°F. Coat 9×5-inch loaf pan with nonstick cooking spray.

2. Beat butter, granulated sugar and brown sugar in large bowl with electric mixer at medium speed until light and fluffy. Beat in eggs, one at a time, scraping down bowl after each addition. Add bananas and vanilla. Beat just until combined.

3. Sift flour, baking powder and salt in small bowl. Gradually beat flour mixture into banana mixture just until combined. Fold in pineapple, coconut and chocolate chips.

4. Spoon batter into prepared pan. Top with walnuts, if desired. Bake 50 minutes or until toothpick inserted into center comes out almost clean. Cool in pan 1 hour; remove from pan.

GREEN GARDEN PIZZA

MAKES
30
SERVINGS

- 2 packages (8 ounces each) refrigerated crescent roll dough
- 12 ounces cream cheese
- 1 cup sour cream
- 2 tablespoons dry ranch salad dressing mix (about ½ package)
- ¾ cup cucumber slices
- 2 cups broccoli florets
- ½ cup carrots slices
- ¾ cup grape tomatoes, cut in half

1. Preheat oven to 375°F. Place dough in single layer in ungreased 15×10×1-inch jelly-roll pan. Press onto bottom and up sides of pan, sealing perforations. Bake 13 to 17 minutes or until brown. Cool on wire rack at least 30 minutes.

2. Beat cream cheese in medium bowl with electric mixer at medium speed until fluffy. Add sour cream and salad dressing mix; beat until blended. Spread over cooled crust.

3. Cut cucumber slices in half. Arrange rows of cucumber slices, broccoli florets, carrot slices and tomato halves on pizza. Cut pizza into 30 rectangles. Serve immediately or cover and refrigerate for up to 24 hours.

COLOR YOUR PIZZA: Try a variety of veggies—bell pepper slices, zucchini noodles, and sugar snap peas. So many choices!

CRISP OATS TRAIL MIX

MAKES
2½
CUPS
(ABOUT
10 SERVINGS)

- 1 cup old-fashioned oats
- ½ cup unsalted shelled pumpkin seeds
- ½ cup dried sweetened cranberries
- ½ cup raisins
- 2 tablespoons maple syrup
- 1 teaspoon canola oil
- ½ teaspoon ground cinnamon
- ¼ teaspoon salt

1. Preheat oven to 325°F. Line baking sheet with heavy-duty foil.

2. Combine all ingredients in large bowl; mix well. Spread on prepared baking sheet.

3. Bake 20 minutes or until oats are lightly browned, stirring halfway through cooking time. Cool completely on baking sheet. Store in airtight container.

CRAZY FOR CRUNCH: The perfect topping for oatmeal, yogurt, or even ice cream!

S'MORE SHAKE

MAKES
4
SERVINGS

- ½ cup graham cracker crumbs
- ¼ cup plus 2 tablespoons fudge topping
- 1 cup marshmallow crème
- ¾ cup milk
- 1 cup vanilla ice cream or frozen yogurt
- Mini graham crackers (optional)
- Additional fudge topping for garnish

COOKIE BASE

Combine graham cracker crumbs and ¼ cup fudge topping in small bowl, mixing with fork until blended. Press about 2 tablespoons mixture into each of 4 (4-ounce) glasses. Reserve any remaining crumb mixture for garnish, if desired. Freeze until ready to serve.

SHAKE

1. Combine marshmallow crème and remaining 2 tablespoons fudge topping in 1-quart glass bowl. Microwave on HIGH 20 to 30 seconds. Stir, mixing until blended and smooth. Gradually whisk in milk.

2. Pour milk mixture in blender; add ice cream. Process until mixture is smooth. Pour over graham cracker base. Garnish with reserved crumb mixture or miniature graham crackers and additional fudge topping.

BANANA PUDDING SMOOTHIE

MAKES

1

SERVING

1 medium frozen banana, broken into pieces

¾ cup milk

1 tablespoon packed light brown sugar

2 teaspoons vanilla

Mini shortbread cookies (optional)

Mini marshmallows, lightly toasted (optional)

1. Combine banana, milk, brown sugar and vanilla in blender; blend until smooth.

2. Pour into glass. Serve with cookies and marshmallows if desired.

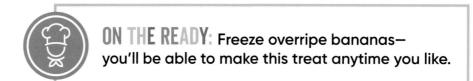

ON THE READY: Freeze overripe bananas—you'll be able to make this treat anytime you like.

MINT CHOCOLATE CHIP MILK SHAKES

MAKES 2 SERVINGS

- 2 cups mint chocolate chip ice cream
- 1 cup milk
- 2 tablespoons whipped topping
- 1 tablespoon mini chocolate chips

1. Combine ice cream and milk in blender; process until smooth.

2. Pour into 2 glasses. Top with whipped topping; sprinkle with chocolate chips.

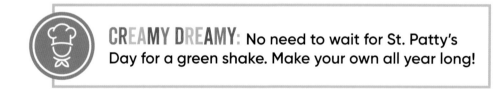

CREAMY DREAMY: No need to wait for St. Patty's Day for a green shake. Make your own all year long!

CHOCOLATE CHOCOLATE COOKIE SHAKE

MAKES
3
SERVINGS

1¼ cups crushed mini crème-filled cookies (about 3 cups cookies), divided

⅓ cup milk, divided

⅛ teaspoon ground cinnamon

1¼ cups vanilla ice cream

¼ cup mini semisweet chocolate morsels

Whipped cream (optional)

Mini crème-filled cookies (optional)

COOKIE BASE
Combine ½ cup cookie crumbs and 1 tablespoon milk in small bowl, mixing with fork until blended. Press 2 tablespoons crumb mixture into each of 3 (4-ounce) glasses; reserve remaining crumb mixture. Place glasses in freezer.

SHAKE

1. Combine cinnamon into ½ cup of the reserved cookie crumbs. Place remaining milk, ice cream, cinnamon crumb mixture and semisweet chocolate chips in blender. Process until smooth.

2. Pour chocolate mixture over cookie base in prepared glasses. Garnish with whipped cream, reserved crumb mixture or miniature crème-filled cookies.

"MOO-VIN" STRAWBERRY MILK SHAKE

MAKES

2

SERVINGS

2 cups (1 pint) vanilla ice cream

1 cup frozen unsweetened strawberries, thawed

¼ cup milk

¼ teaspoon vanilla

Decorator sprinkles (optional)

1. Combine ice cream, strawberries, milk and vanilla in blender. Process until smooth.

2. Pour into 2 small glasses. Top with sprinkles, if desired. Serve immediately.

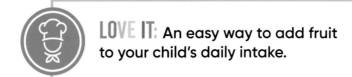

LOVE IT: An easy way to add fruit to your child's daily intake.

ROOT BEER BARREL SHAKE

MAKES

1

SERVING

- ½ cup vanilla frozen yogurt
- 1 cup root beer
- ½ teaspoon vanilla
- Whipped cream
- Root beer-flavored hard candy, crushed (optional)

1. Place glass mug in freezer at least 1 hour (or longer) before serving time, if desired.

2. Combine ice cream, root beer and vanilla in blender. Process about 10 seconds or until smooth and mixed. Pour in frozen mug or glass. Top with whipped cream and candy, if desired.

FIZZY FUN: When carbonation from the root beer mixes with the ice cream, you get bubbles and foam—so fun to sip and drink!

COLD AS MICE

MAKES
6
SERVINGS

1 quart (4 cups) vanilla ice cream or frozen yogurt

12 chocolate sandwich cookies

Candy-coated chocolate pieces

Chocolate sprinkles

1. Place 1 scoop vanilla ice cream in each of 6 small serving dishes.

2. Press 2 cookies into scoop of ice cream for ears.

3. Press candies into ice cream for eyes and nose. Arrange chocolate sprinkles at sides of nose for whiskers.

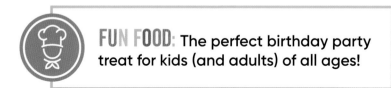

FUN FOOD: The perfect birthday party treat for kids (and adults) of all ages!

OVER THE RAINBOW

MAKES

3

SERVINGS

1½ **cups orange juice**

⅓ **cup rainbow sherbet**

½ **cup club soda**

Additional rainbow sherbet for garnish (optional)

1. Combine juice and ⅓ cup sherbet in blender. Process until smooth. Pour into glasses; add club soda.

2. Top with additional sherbet, if desired.

EASY TO IMPRESS: Dip the edge of the glass in water, then colored sugars before filling. So festive!

BRING ON THE SWEETS

ICE CREAM CONE CUPCAKES

24 flat-bottomed ice cream cones

1 package (about 15 ounces) white cake mix, plus ingredients to prepare mix

2 tablespoons colored nonpareils

Prepared vanilla and chocolate frostings

Additional nonpareils and decors

1. Preheat oven to 350°F. Stand ice cream cones in 13×9-inch baking pan or muffin cups.

2. Prepare cake mix according to package directions; stir in 2 tablespoons nonpareils. Spoon batter evenly into cones.

3. Bake 20 minutes or until toothpick inserted into centers comes out clean. Remove to wire racks; cool completely.

4. Frost cupcakes and decorate as desired.

NOTE: These cupcakes are best served the day they are made.

161

BURGER BLISS

MAKES
2
DOZEN
SANDWICH
COOKIES

BUNS

- 1 package (about 16 ounces) refrigerated sugar cookie dough
- ½ cup creamy peanut butter
- ⅓ cup all-purpose flour
- ¼ cup packed brown sugar
- ½ teaspoon vanilla

  Beaten egg white and sesame seeds (optional)

BURGERS

- ½ (16-ounce) package refrigerated sugar cookie dough*
- 3 tablespoons unsweetened cocoa powder
- 2 tablespoons packed brown sugar
- ½ teaspoon vanilla

  Red, yellow and green decorating icings

*Reserve remaining dough for another use.

1. Preheat oven to 350°F. Grease cookie sheets.

2. For buns, let 1 package dough stand at room temperature 15 minutes. Combine 1 package dough, peanut butter, flour, ¼ cup brown sugar and ½ teaspoon vanilla in large bowl; beat with electric mixer at medium speed until well blended. Shape into 48 (1-inch) balls; place 2 inches apart on prepared cookie sheets.

3. Bake 14 minutes or until lightly browned. Brush half of cookies with egg white and sprinkle with sesame seeds after 10 minutes, if desired. Cool on cookie sheets 2 minutes. Remove to wire racks; cool completely.

4. For burgers, let ½ package dough stand at room temperature 15 minutes. Beat dough, cocoa, 2 tablespoons brown sugar and ½ teaspoon vanilla in medium bowl with electric mixer at medium speed until well blended. Shape into 24 (1-inch) balls; place 2 inches apart on prepared cookie sheets. Flatten to ¼-inch thickness.

5. Bake 12 minutes or until set. Cool on cookie sheets 2 minutes. Remove to wire racks; cool completely.

6. To assemble, use icing to attach burgers to flat side of 24 buns. Pipe red, yellow and green icings on burgers to resemble condiments. Top with remaining buns.

KITTY KAT

MAKES
12
SERVINGS

1 package (about 16 ounces) carrot cake mix, plus ingredients to prepare mix

1 container (16 ounces) cream cheese frosting

Red and yellow food coloring

2 cupcakes

¼ cup chocolate sprinkles

Assorted round and heart-shaped candies

Black licorice string

1. Preheat oven to 350°F. Prepare and bake cake mix according to package directions for 2 (8- or 9-inch) round cakes. Cool completely.

2. Blend frosting and food coloring in medium bowl until desired shade of orange reached. Place 1 cake layer on serving plate; spread with frosting. Top with second cake layer; frost top and side of cake.

3. Cut ⅜ inch from three sides of each cupcake to create triangles to resemble ears. Position ears next to cake and frost. Use tines of fork to make frosting resemble fur as shown in photo. Scatter sprinkles around edge of cake and in center of ears.

4. Decorate cat face with assorted candies. Cut licorice strings into 2-inch lengths for mouth. Position candles on cake to resemble whiskers or use additional licorice strings.

ROCKY ROAD PUDDING

MAKES
6
SERVINGS

- **5 tablespoons unsweetened cocoa powder**
- **½ cup sugar, divided**
- **3 tablespoons cornstarch**
- **⅛ teaspoon salt**
- **2½ cups milk**
- **2 egg yolks, beaten**
- **2 teaspoons vanilla**
- **1 cup mini marshmallows**
- **¼ cup chopped walnuts, toasted***

*To toast walnuts, spread in single layer in heavy skillet. Cook over medium heat 3 minutes or until nuts are fragrant, stirring frequently.

1. Combine cocoa, ¼ cup sugar, cornstarch and salt in small saucepan; stir until well blended. Stir in milk until smooth. Cook over medium-high heat about 10 minutes or until mixture thickens and begins to boil, stirring constantly.

2. Whisk ½ cup hot milk mixture into beaten egg yolks in small bowl. Pour mixture back into saucepan; cook over medium heat 10 minutes or until mixture reaches 160°F, whisking constantly. Remove from heat; stir in vanilla.

3. Place plastic wrap on surface of pudding. Refrigerate about 20 minutes or until slightly cooled. Stir in remaining ¼ cup sugar. Spoon pudding into 6 dessert dishes; top with marshmallows and walnuts.

GOOD TO KNOW: The term "rocky road" was created to make a "rocky" time in history easier to handle by combining treats like marshmallows and walnuts.

LEFTOVER CANDY BARK

MAKES

3

POUNDS

3 cups chopped leftover chocolate candy

2 packages (12 ounces each) white chocolate chips

1 package (10 ounces) peanut butter chips

1. Line 13×9-inch baking pan with parchment paper. Spread candy in prepared baking pan and freeze at least 1 hour.

2. Melt white chocolate and peanut butter chips in large microwavable bowl on HIGH at 45-second intervals, stirring after each interval, until melted and smooth, about 5 minutes total. Towards the end, check every 20 to 30 seconds. Stir in 2½ cups candy and spread evenly in same parchment-lined baking pan; sprinkle with remaining ½ cup candy. Refrigerate about 1 hour or until firm. Break into pieces.

NOTE: For thinner bark, use a sheet pan instead of a 13×9-inch baking pan.

CHOP IT UP: Use all types of candy you have on hand— what a great way to use up all the extra pieces!

DOUGHNUT HOLE FONDUE

MAKES

6

SERVINGS

¾ cup whipping cream

1 cup bittersweet or semisweet chocolate chips

1 tablespoon butter

½ teaspoon vanilla

12 to 16 doughnut holes

Sliced fresh fruit, such as pineapple, bananas, strawberries, melon and oranges

1. Heat cream in small saucepan until bubbles form around edge. Remove from heat. Add chocolate; let stand 2 minutes or until softened. Add butter and vanilla; whisk until smooth. Keep warm in fondue pot or transfer to serving bowl.

2. Serve with doughnut holes and fruit.

EASY TO DO: Make your own doughnut holes—1 can refrigerated biscuit dough (cut each biscuit into quarters), dip in melted butter, roll in cinnamon-sugar, then bake at 350°F for 18 to 20 minutes.

CUPCAKE SLIDERS

MAKES
18
CUPCAKES

2 cups all-purpose flour

2½ teaspoons baking powder

½ teaspoon salt

1 cup milk

½ teaspoon vanilla

1½ cups sugar

½ cup (1 stick) butter, softened

3 eggs

1¼ cups chocolate hazelnut spread or milk chocolate frosting

Confetti sprinkles (optional)

1. Preheat oven to 350°F. Spray 18 standard (2½-inch) muffin cups with nonstick cooking spray.

2. Whisk flour, baking powder and salt in medium bowl. Combine milk and vanilla in measuring cup. Beat sugar and butter in large bowl with electric mixer at medium speed about 3 minutes or until creamy. Add eggs, one at a time, beating well after each addition. Add flour mixture alternately with milk mixture, beating until well blended. Spoon batter into prepared muffin cups, filling about three-fourths full.

3. Bake 18 to 20 minutes or until toothpick inserted into centers comes out clean. Cool in pans 10 minutes. Remove to wire racks; cool completely.

4. Cut off edges of cupcakes to form squares. Cut cupcakes in half crosswise. Spread each bottom half with about 1 tablespoon chocolate hazelnut spread; top with sprinkles, if desired. Replace tops of cupcakes.

CANDY BAR TAFFY APPLE SALAD

MAKES ABOUT

8

CUPS

2 apples, chopped

2 cups miniature marshmallows

2 cups thawed frozen whipped topping

1 cup chopped chocolate candy bars

½ cup salted peanuts

Combine apples, marshmallows, whipped topping, candy bars and peanuts in large bowl; stir to blend. Refrigerate 1 hour before serving.

SO ADDICTING: Kids will eat up this tasty salad—it tastes like a taffy apple!

VARIATION: To use a muffin pan instead of ramekins, double all ingredients. Spray 11 standard (2½-inch) muffin pan cups with nonstick cooking spray. Use 7 biscuit pieces in each muffin cup, layering with chocolate chips and mini marshmallows as directed in step 3. Bake as directed in step 4. Loosen edges of muffins with knife immediately after baking; remove muffins to serving plate. Makes 11 muffins.

COOKIE CRUMB SUNDAE

MAKES
12 TO 14
SERVINGS

1 package (18¼ ounces) chocolate crème-filled sandwich cookies

4 cups milk, divided

1 package (4-serving size) cheesecake instant pudding and pie filling mix

1 package (4-serving size) chocolate fudge instant pudding and pie filling mix

1 container (8 ounces) frozen whipped topping, thawed

12 to 14 maraschino cherries, drained

1. Place cookies in large resealable food storage bag; crush with rolling pin. Place three fourths of crumbs in bottom of 13×9-inch baking pan or large serving bowl.

2. Combine 2 cups milk and cheesecake pudding mix in large bowl. Prepare according to package directions. Pour pudding evenly over cookie crumbs.

3. Repeat with remaining 2 cups milk and chocolate pudding mix. Pour evenly over cheesecake pudding.

4. Spread whipped topping over pudding. Sprinkle remaining cookie crumbs over whipped topping. Top with maraschino cherries. Chill 1 hour before serving.

EAT UP: For parties and picnics, make the dessert in individual disposable clean plastic cups. Decorate with festive colored sprinkles.

COLORFUL CATERPILLAR CUPCAKES

MAKES
20
CUPCAKES

1 package (about 18 ounces) vanilla cake mix

1¼ cups water

3 eggs

⅓ cup vegetable oil

Assorted food coloring

Buttercream Frosting (recipe follows)

Assorted candies, candy-coated chocolate pieces, red string licorice and lollipops

Gummy worms

1. Preheat oven to 350°F. Line 20 standard (2½-inch) muffin cups with paper baking cups.*

2. Beat cake mix, water, eggs and oil in large bowl with electric mixer at low speed 30 seconds. Beat at medium speed 2 minutes or until well blended. Divide batter among 5 bowls; add different food coloring to each bowl, a few drops at a time, until desired shades are reached. Spoon batter into prepared muffin cups, filling three-fourths full.

3. Bake 20 minutes or until toothpick inserted into centers comes out clean. Cool in pans 10 minutes. Remove to wire racks; cool completely.

4. Prepare Buttercream Frosting. Set aside 2 cupcakes for caterpillar head.

5. Frost remaining cupcakes. Place 1 cupcake on its side at edge of serving plate. Place second cupcake on its side in front of first cupcake; arrange remaining cupcakes, alternating colors, in row to create body of caterpillar.

METRIC CONVERSION CHART

VOLUME MEASUREMENTS (dry)

$^1/_8$ teaspoon = 0.5 mL
$^1/_4$ teaspoon = 1 mL
$^1/_2$ teaspoon = 2 mL
$^3/_4$ teaspoon = 4 mL
1 teaspoon = 5 mL
1 tablespoon = 15 mL
2 tablespoons = 30 mL
$^1/_4$ cup = 60 mL
$^1/_3$ cup = 75 mL
$^1/_2$ cup = 125 mL
$^2/_3$ cup = 150 mL
$^3/_4$ cup = 175 mL
1 cup = 250 mL
2 cups = 1 pint = 500 mL
3 cups = 750 mL
4 cups = 1 quart = 1 L

VOLUME MEASUREMENTS (fluid)

1 fluid ounce (2 tablespoons) = 30 mL
4 fluid ounces ($^1/_2$ cup) = 125 mL
8 fluid ounces (1 cup) = 250 mL
12 fluid ounces (1$^1/_2$ cups) = 375 mL
16 fluid ounces (2 cups) = 500 mL

WEIGHTS (mass)

$^1/_2$ ounce = 15 g
1 ounce = 30 g
3 ounces = 90 g
4 ounces = 120 g
8 ounces = 225 g
10 ounces = 285 g
12 ounces = 360 g
16 ounces = 1 pound = 450 g

DIMENSIONS

$^1/_{16}$ inch = 2 mm
$^1/_8$ inch = 3 mm
$^1/_4$ inch = 6 mm
$^1/_2$ inch = 1.5 cm
$^3/_4$ inch = 2 cm
1 inch = 2.5 cm

OVEN TEMPERATURES

250°F = 120°C
275°F = 140°C
300°F = 150°C
325°F = 160°C
350°F = 180°C
375°F = 190°C
400°F = 200°C
425°F = 220°C
450°F = 230°C

BAKING PAN SIZES

Utensil	Size in Inches/Quarts	Metric Volume	Size in Centimeters
Baking or Cake Pan (square or rectangular)	8×8×2	2 L	20×20×5
	9×9×2	2.5 L	23×23×5
	12×8×2	3 L	30×20×5
	13×9×2	3.5 L	33×23×5
Loaf Pan	8×4×3	1.5 L	20×10×7
	9×5×3	2 L	23×13×7
Round Layer Cake Pan	8×1½	1.2 L	20×4
	9×1½	1.5 L	23×4
Pie Plate	8×1¼	750 mL	20×3
	9×1¼	1 L	23×3
Baking Dish or Casserole	1 quart	1 L	—
	1½ quart	1.5 L	—
	2 quart	2 L	—